MY NAME IS KAS

Linda S. Blaz

authorHOUSE®

AuthorHouse™
1663 Liberty Drive, Suite 200
Bloomington, IN 47403
www.authorhouse.com
Phone: 1-800-839-8640

First published by AuthorHouse 6/8/2009

ISBN: 978-1-4389-1405-3 (sc)

Library of Congress Control Number: 2008908429

Printed in the United States of America
Bloomington, Indiana

This book is printed on acid-free paper.

OTHER BOOKS BY LINDA:
THE ZESTFUL LIFE (Enjoy your life)
THE DIVORCE BOOK (How to cope with divorce)
Website: Authorhouse.com

THIS BOOK IS DEDICATED TO:
Jami K.Osteen
and all her animals.

Contents

INTRODUCTION

My name is Kas and this is my story. I was born on a big horse ranch. It was a fun and carefree life. We were a social family and everyone on the ranch knew us. I had lots of friends and family and enjoyed romping around the pastures.

The ranch folks were a happy, kind, and caring family. They took good care of us and we enjoyed our interactions with them.

I was always looking for ways to have fun. After awhile my friends started to call me, KAS. One of the fillies told me that my nickname came from Casanova who was a famous lover. Wow! I knew I had quite a way with the fillies, but Casanova. I hoped he was a caring and suave guy. I decided to enjoy my nickname and new reputation. I was quite the popular stallion on the ranch. I liked to romp and folic around with my friends and family, but especially with the fillies. I could always be found all over the fields, high stepping, chatting, and having fun.

My life was filled with friends, family, and fun. I had a mighty good time. We all had great fun on the ranch. I was always flirting and looking for fun. I was a proud young man, just like my Daddy. He liked to flirt too. Mom understood and knew it was all in fun and the way of the stallion. However, we ended up with a big family. Our reunions were a ball. We had lots of friends too. Everyone got along, and we had a great times together. I never got married as I was having too much fun with all the fillies. We were together for a long time on our home ranch. It was enjoyable, fun, full of laughter and good times.

I was always a curious fellow. I learned what the home ranch people called "tricks". It was fun. I wanted to check out new places, see different things, and try new ideas. I learned how to open the garbage cans and we had fun throwing the lids around the pastures. The ranch people would lecture me, but they would laugh when they thought I wasn't looking. I found many interesting things in the trash. I even figured out how to open the gates and doors.

Then one day, after many tries, I figured out how to open the food containers in the barn. Now that was a big day! I would sunder into the barn when the ranch people were busy elsewhere. I'd help myself to cookies, hay, alfalfa, and anything else I could find to eat. Snacks are good! Soon my buddies realized something was going on and followed me into the barn. They appreciated my new skills and joined in the snack party. When I'd head for the barn, they'd start yelling, "There goes Kas, let's party!"

We were content on the ranch. We settled into our daily routine with fun, flirting, parties, and romping all over the big ranch. Times were good. Life was carefree and enjoyable in every way.

Time passed and suddenly in one day, everything changed. We were shocked and afraid. Our lives would never be the same again.

PART#1

WHAT IS HAPPENING??

Suddenly out of nowhere, big horse trailers arrived at the farm. The cowboys herded many of my friends and relatives into the trailers and drove away. Soon other trailers arrived. These trailers also brought many new youngsters to our home farm. These young ones were immature, inexperienced, had little to say, and knew nothing. They acted silly. I didn't know where the cowboys got them, but our home farm youngsters never acted that way.

These colts didn't even know how to have fun. They were going to need a lot of teaching. I did not understand what was happening. Nobody seemed to know. The home ranch people said nothing. Strange cowboys silently loaded and unloaded the trailers and they said nothing either.

Finally, we heard that our friends and relatives went to a variety of other places to get jobs. I wasn't sure what would happen next. I asked Mom and Dad. They explained that after a certain age many horses move away from their home farms. Sometimes older horses are sent out on their own to get jobs. They explained my turn to get a job might come soon too. I was shocked. I was happy on my home ranch. I liked to have fun in the fields with my friends. I was not sure I wanted any part of this job idea.

However, soon another horse trailer arrived. This time the cowboy told me that it was my turn to get into the trailer. Mom and Dad were sad and so was I. They told me I was a man now and I was going to be on my own. We all cried. I was a horse who liked to be with his friends and family. I wanted to stay on my home farm. I felt I was still needed on the ranch. Those colts desperately needed training. I was the man for that job, but no one asked me. I could have given them lessons in life and taught them Kas proverbs.

I was upset, but it didn't matter what I thought at all. Off we went traveling far into the night. The trailer drove for miles and miles. I noticed the sky was getting darker and darker. Then we stopped. We stayed still for awhile and I fell asleep. Then suddenly the engine roared and off we went again.

In a short while, we made a turn, slowed down, traveled down a different road, and stopped. Different cowboys got us out of the trailer. We were quickly put into individual stalls in a big barn. There seemed to be many horses already in the barn. They were making lots of noise, but I couldn't see anyone else. I was upset again. I did not want to be in a barn.

I was use to being out in the fields and not staying in a barn. No one said anything to us. After awhile, a fellow across the way yelled to me, "Hi! I'm Gus. What's your name?" I told him that I was Kas. He was friendly and helpful. Gus explained that this was a training farm for riders. I was happy to meet a new friend in this strange place. Now I didn't feel so alone. We were in small stalls. When I looked out, I saw a long hallway with lots of other stalls. I missed Mom, Dad, my friends, and relatives. I missed the pastures of my home ranch already.

I felt better when the new people brought us food. I realized I was starved. They gave us fresh water too. Gus said that the food was always plentiful and good at the training place. I was glad to hear that news. After we finished eating, Gus explained our job on the ranch.

Gus said that different people would be riding us every day. He said there was always a wide range of people. Some were good, but most were beginners. The experienced riders went to another training ranch. I told Gus I didn't think I would like this job. First of all, it sounded boring. Secondly, I wanted to be in the pastures, not in the barn. Third, beginners are too unpredictable. Fourth, I wanted to be with family and friends. I wondered how I was chosen for this job.

I remembered my home people saying I was an easy ride. They said it was a compliment, but now I was going to have a boring job. I was eager to get out in the fields and check out the place. I also wanted to meet other fellows and fillies too, but the people just kept us in the barn.

In a few days, the people put riding gear on us. I was upset again. I pounded the ground, snorted, and jumped around as I tried to get my message across to them. I did not want their job. I was sure there must be a job that would be more fun than this one. I was bored already. The people ignored my protests and nobody cared what I thought about the job.

The people lined us up, one after another, in a long line. Then a rider got up on each of us and off we went for our boring day. Gus was right we sure got a variety of people coming each day to go riding. Some riders wanted to trot slow, others wanted to poke, and others were totally confused. All in all, the job was still boring. Gus would keep saying that it takes all kinds to make up the world. Other wise, things really would be totally boring. He was right. Variety was good and our job did have a little variety from time to time.

Once in awhile, a person would cause us to laugh and laugh, especially when they knew nothing about riding. We would get the giggles. Some people should not choose riding horses as a hobby.

Day after day, we'd line up for the riders and go around the pastures. Sometimes, they'd take longer rides and stop for a lunch break. The riders would relax and not be in any hurry. We liked those rides. These rides gave us time to chat with each other, have some fun, and even flirt.

In the evenings, Gus and I would chat, laugh, and entertain each other. If it wasn't for Gus, I would have gone bonkers or wacky. It was great to talk with someone and enjoy a friendship. Gus was a good friend and I felt fortunate to have met him. I decided to adopt him as my brother. Gus liked the idea. He said we would be buddies forever. Gus missed being part of a family too.

We would also talk to the other horses around us. We would yell to each other up and down the long hallway. We all made the best of the situation and tried to enjoy our evenings In the barn. We walked in line all day and did the best we could to enjoy our evenings together.

PART #2

WHAT'S NEXT??

Time seemed to pass slowly, but we got into our daily routine. We usually got up just before sun rise when the people brought us breakfast and fresh water.

One day we awoke from our nights sleep and realized we had overslept. This had never happened before and we were surprised. The sun was shining brightly. The place was quiet. We yelled and yelled. Nothing happened and no one came into the barn. No one had any idea about what was happening. Where were the people? Gus and others began to worry. They wondered what was going to happen? Gus told me that if all the riding people were gone, we were in big trouble.

Gus suggested laughingly that maybe a space ship took the people away. Everyone laughed. I said that I hoped the space ship had left us some food. Someone else said they wanted to go on the space ship too as they wanted to be the first horse in space. We all started laughing again. Then everyone started yelling that they wanted to go on the space ship. We were laughing and laughing. It made us feel better. We were trying to keep a positive outlook. Gus and others were starting to worry again. I told them to relax, we'd be okay, but I was worried too.

We waited and waited, but no one came to the barn. The food in our stalls was running low. Gus wanted to know why the riding people would just leave us? He wondered why they didn't leave us with more food or take us to another farm? We just shook our heads in disbelief and bewilderment. I felt this situation was something we would never be able to understand, because their behavior was heartless and cruel.

We were sad and worried.

We missed our families and friends back at our home farms. However, we had made new friends and we would stick together. We were truly thankful for each other. I knew we would do our best until somehow help would come for us.

I decided something had to be done quickly to find food. We had little food left in our stalls and we needed water too. Gus tried to open his stall door and many others also tried to open their doors. They did not succeed and everyone was getting upset. I decided it was up to me to solve this problem. I told everyone to relax and I'd give my door a try. I used the tricks I had learned back at my home farm. Little did I know that my fun tricks would come in handy in such a difficult situation.

I worked on the latch for awhile. Then suddenly I got it open. I pushed the door and it swung open wide. I trotted out of the stall. (I had become quite good at opening latches, gates, boxes, garbage cans, and doors). Everyone cheered. I was excited and relieved.

I then let Gus out of his stall. I showed him how to open the latches. Then we both hurried to let everybody else out of their stalls. We all trotted eagerly out of the barn into the yard. It felt good to be out of the barn, but the place looked deserted. It was just what we suspected. We were all alone. No one was there. We were happy to be out of the barn. We played and romped. We checked out every corner of the pastures. The fences were secure, so we were limited in where we could go to find food. There was some grass, but much of the fields were dirt.

We started to look for food which had become our major concern and worry. We did find a small pond where we could get water and that was a relief.

In a shed, I found cookies, treats, food, and little cube things. I knew these wouldn't last long as horses are big eaters. I suggested that each of us eat just a little each day because that would make the food last longer. We had no idea when, or if, anyone would show up at the farm. Days and nights passed. We tried not to feel hopeless. We tried to keep our spirits up and think positive, but food was running low. No one came and we began to feel afraid. I found a few meals in the garbage cans, but things looked very bleak.

Each day we were getting weaker and hungrier. I kept encouraging everyone, but we had run out of ideas and had no where else to turn for help. Things just got steadily worse.

At first, we would run and play. We were overjoyed to be out of the barn. We thought surely someone would come back to the farm and rescue us, but no one came.

Sometimes cars would drive by the farm. No one stopped or even slowed down or even looked our way as they zoomed by us. It was like we were invisible, no one noticed, or cared. Some became depressed, others angry, and others were too weak to even stand. We waited and waited and waited. We were in a severe crisis. We could not think of anything else to help us. We even thought of storming the fences, but we were much too weak. I was also concerned that some of us would be seriously injured. We waited and waited and waited.

PART #3

HELP!!!!

We had just about given up hope that anyone would find us and, suddenly, all kinds of cars drove into the yard. People piled out of the cars. Most of them were dressed in uniforms. They seemed upset and went all over the place checking every inch of the farm. We were hoping they'd bring us food and stay with us.

Gus said that some of the people were police. He'd seen police before at his home farm when they came to ride horses. Gus had several friends who had jobs with the police mounted patrol. They had told Gus how much they liked their jobs. They got lots of attention, good food, went many places, saw lots of people, and each had their own special police person to ride them. Now that sounded like a good job and not boring at all.

Gus and I realized that we were badly out of shape. We were tired, hungry, and feeling miserable. We had been holding out hope, but now we knew for sure we had been on the verge of complete disaster. We were relieved as we felt things were finally going to be better for all of us.

Soon big horse trailers arrived. The cowboys loaded everyone into the trailers and we drove away. We were hopeful, but fearful and wondering what would happen next.

We rode for a couple days and nights. We had plenty of food and water. We were hungry and thirsty. We were still tired and weak. I looked at Gus. I was shocked. He looked awful. He was just skin and bones. I could see his rib bones. I hardly recognized him. I knew we were in bad shape, but now that we were in the trailer I realized how bad he looked. I was worried about him. Gus said I didn't look so good either.

PART #4

THE RESCUE FARM

On the third day, we drove into a big yard. The trailers stopped, the cowboys got us out, and led us all into a big pasture. We were excited and relieved when we saw the open pastures. The fields were just like our home farms. There was a big barn, and we were allowed to come and go as we pleased. We had plenty of food and water.

Gus said he heard the cowboys talking and they said this was a rescue farm. Gus said that animals come to rescue places after they have received heartless, neglectful, and cruel care. Animals stay at the rescue places until they are well again. Sometimes the rescue place becomes their homes, other times they get adopted, and get new homes.

Gus and I were glad all of us had been rescued. We were all badly in need of help. We were thankful that a rescue place existed for horses like us. We didn't want to think about what might have happened to us without a rescue farm.

I was still worried about Gus. The Vet Lady took Gus to a special barn. She said he needed special attention and care. Then I was even more worried about my buddy, Gus.

I was feeling better every day, so I was able to stay in the pastures. I didn't need any special care. The Vet Lady gave us all check ups, shots, and medicine. The rescue people seemed to care about us. We were enjoying romping and playing in the field. I was even able to do a little flirting again. We had to take it easy at first as we slowly regained our strength.

There was plenty of other horses in the fields. Many

were friendly and happy to see us. There were all kinds of colors, sizes, shapes, old, young. Some of the horses seemed to have big problems. I think some had been injured and had to be careful; others had to have their own private play areas. I was doing fine, but missed Gus and worried about him.

The rescue Boss Lady and her helpers were always talking to us and checking on us to be sure we were doing okay. We had plenty of food, hay, grass, and treats too. I knew they would take care of Gus, but he looked very bad. I think we were rescued just in time. At least, I hoped that was true. I wanted to visit Gus, but the hospital unit was in another pasture and fenced off from visitors. I keep thinking about how awful Gus looked when they took him to the hospital for special care.

I knew that worrying never helps, but I felt I wanted somehow to help Gus and I knew I could not do a thing. I hoped he knew I was thinking of him and that we were buddies forever.

It seemed to take a long time, but one day I looked up and there was Gus. He looked so much better, almost like his old self. We were excited and happy to see each other. I had been so worried about Gus. I was thrilled to have my friend feeling fine again.

Now we could enjoy the farm together. I showed him all around the farm. We romped and played. This was the first time we could really have fun together in the pastures, not locked up in that riding place barn, or sick. We enjoyed each other's company. Gus and I were happy and grateful for our new home. We were overjoyed to be together and having fun. We even made some new friends. Now that Gus was well. I was able to relax and really feel safe and happy. We were settling into a comfortable routine and enjoying ourselves.

The rescue helpers gave us carrots, treats, and took good care of us. The Feet Man came and fixed our feet. We were feeling safe and happy. However, I did notice I would get short of breath and wheeze. Gus said we were getting to be senior citizens, but we were young at heart. I was almost back to my handsome, proud, flirting self. We laughed and laughed when I told Gus that everyone at my home farm called me, Kasanova. We romped and played in the fields at our own pace. We made new friends, became more content, and settled into a carefree, easy going routine. I thought Gus and I would be buddies, romp the fields together, and live a happy life at the rescue farm. We talked about finding an adoptive family where we could be together, but realized that would probably be impossible. We were thankful and happy to be together, plus living at a fine farm.

PART #5

ADOPTION

One day, Boss Lady brought a tall, sturdy built, lady to meet Gus. Boss Lady and the Tall Lady talked about her visiting and riding Gus. We got to know Tall Lady as she came often to ride, groom, and spend time with Gus. She was kind, gentle, and an experienced rider. She was nice to me too. Gus enjoyed her visits and so did I. Tall Lady's visits went on for quite awhile. She and Gus developed a close relationship. She had an upbeat and fun personality. She was friendly with me too. She could tell Gus and I were close buddies.

Then Gus said he had to talk to me about something serious. Gus explained that he was happy and sad. He said Tall Lady wanted to adopt him and take him to her farm to be a member of her family. This made him happy, but he didn't want to leave me by myself at the rescue farm. Gus said Tall Lady liked me too, but she could only take one of us. Gus said she felt sad, but only had room for one horse at her farm. Gus and I cried. I knew Gus and I wanted to be together, but I also realized Gus wanted a family. I told Gus he had to go with Tall Lady as this was a rescue farm. I couldn't let him pass up the chance to have a real home farm. I would miss him, but I knew he would be happy with Tall Lady. I told Gus we would always be buddies, being adopted by Tall Lady would never change that fact. I told him that we'd work out some way for us to see each other again. After we talked for awhile, he felt better and was happy about the adoption. Later in the week, Boss Lady approved the adoption. Gus was excited. He raced around telling everyone goodbye. I was happy for him and felt sure we'd see each other again.

Part #6

GUS FINDS A HOME,
KAS FINDS A HOME TOO

Gus went happily to his new adopted family and I was glad for him. Yet, I was sad for myself. I missed Gus. I was use to having him around all the time. We did everything together. It was hard when my close buddy moved away. I kept busy playing and romping with my other friends, but It just wasn't the same. I knew I had to make the best of the situation, but it was not easy for me. I knew the important thing was that Gus was happy and I wanted what was best for him.

One day, I was standing in the pasture talking and kidding with my friends. We looked up and saw two people coming our way. They stood and watched us for awhile. Then Boss Lady came up to them and they all talked together while watching us. We were curious ourselves. I was surprised when the Boss Lady came over to me. She took me over to them. Boss Lady said that they were mother and daughter. The Young Girl rubbed my back, talked to me, and gave me a treat. She seemed nice. Her mother smiled, but was quiet. It was fun to have visitors.

In a few days, the Young Girl and her mother came to visit me again. The Young Girl brushed me, talked to me, and rode me around the farm. Then the Young Girl started to come to visit me every few days. She was nice to me and I enjoyed having a regular visitor. She looked quite young and I wasn't sure she would keep coming to visit. I thought she probably would rather play and romp with her own friends. However, she did keep coming to see me.

One morning I was relaxing in the pasture, I looked up

and I saw Young Lady. Then I noticed that her mother came along with her this time. Boss Lady joined them and they came over to the field to see me. I didn't know it then, but my life was going to change again.

Boss Lady said Young Girl had gotten the permission of her mother to adopt me. I was going home with them today. I was shocked. I thought Young Girl was only a visitor, but now I'd be a member of their family. Now I really knew how Gus felt when he got his new adoptive family. I was thrilled. I wanted to be able to tell Gus. I knew he'd be happy for me. The horse trailer arrived for my trip to my new home. The driver was Cowboy Andy. I could tell he knew what he was doing and everything went smoothly.

Gus had told me when you are adopted you become a member of that new family. He said it's just like you were born on their home farm. Now it is your family too. He said you have new relatives and will be part of all family reunions.

Before Cowboy Andy arrived, Boss Lady noticed I wanted to go, but I was nervous about leaving the rescue farm. She told me I could come back if things didn't work out there. She said I would always have a home with her and the helpers at the rescue farm. I wondered about Gus and his adoption. Boss Lady told me Gus was having a great time at his new home. She said she hoped I would too. Boss Lady explained she'd come to visit me regularly to be sure I was okay and liked the place. She also said the Vet Lady would come to check on me too. I felt much better and off I went with Cowboy Andy.

I quickly settled comfortably into my new home. I liked the place. Young Girl took care of me everyday. We had fun together. I had plenty of food and water. I had my own pasture and could come and go out of the barn. I was enjoying myself.

Everything went fine for awhile, then slowly Young Lady came less and less to see me. Then she stopped coming and I was all alone. I began to worry. I remembered what happened at the riding farm.

Suddenly, the Vet Lady came to see me. She checked me and gave me a shot. She seemed upset. She made a call on her cell phone. Soon rescue Boss Lady arrived. She was upset too. They said I looked neglected. The Vet Lady said Young Girl was not taking good care of me anymore. She said maybe the girl was too young and had too many other interests. I was relieved the Boss Lady and Vet Lady had both come to see me.

Boss Lady was not at all happy about my situation. She was upset and raised her voice. Suddenly, my life changed again. Soon Cowboy Andy and his horse trailer arrived. Boss Lady said I was going back home to the rescue farm with her. I was glad I would not be alone anymore and would be at a good, safe home again. I got into the horse trailer and Cowboy Andy took me back to the rescue farm.

Vet Lady checked me again and said I'd be fine. I felt safe at the rescue farm. Boss Lady and her helpers took good care of us all. I felt grateful that Vet Lady and Boss Lady kept a close check on me. I was glad I didn't have to go through another experience like the riding farm disaster.

I was sad that things didn't work out at the adoptive home. I had hoped to have a family. I liked the rescue farm, Boss Lady, and her helpers, but I almost had my own family. I missed Gus and my friends and family at the home farm. I wanted to be part of a family again.

I thought maybe I was becoming an ugly horse and no one would want me any more. I was afraid I'd end up at the glue factory or become dog food. Boss Lady said I could stay with her forever. She was nice, but I realized I wanted a family. I didn't feel like talking, playing, romping, or even flirting anymore. I just stayed by myself. My friends tried to help and encourage me, but nothing seemed to help. I was a sad and depressed horse.

PART #8

WILL THERE BE A FAMILY FOR KAS?

Time passed and one morning when I awoke, I realized the sun was shining brightly and the weather was perfect. Right then, I decided to stop feeling sorry for myself. I knew the rescue farm was a nice place to live. I had friends here, wide open pastures, and nice people. I began romping, playing, and flirting again in my proud senior citizen way. Boss Lady and her helpers took good care of me and I was doing fine. I put the idea of having my own family aside and enjoyed myself at the farm.

Then one day, Boss Lady brought a Little Lady to meet me. Little Lady was kind and friendly. I liked her right away and she seemed to like me. I wasn't sure what would happen next, but my life was about to change again.

Little Lady started to visit me regularly at the rescue farm. Boss Lady said that Little Lady wanted to get to know me. I liked the idea of having her as a regular visitor. I was happy and, sure enough, she came to see me on a regular basis. She was gentle, caring, friendly, yet firm. She was going to be in charge and she made this fact quite clear. There was something about her that I liked a lot. Sometimes, we'd just walk around together, or visit the other horses. We had fun just hanging around together. She would bush, groom, and feed me. I enjoyed her visits. I felt Little Lady and I were becoming good friends. I began to hope that she felt the same way.

Suddenly to my surprise one sunny afternoon, Boss Lady took me aside and explained that Little Lady wanted to adopt me. She even wanted to take me to her home and become a member of her family. I was thrilled, but scared. I began to worry as I didn't want to be disappointed again.

I had secretly hoped that this would happen, but I was afraid to think about the possibilities of adoption. I wanted to be part of a family, but I didn't want to get my hopes up again. I decided to enjoy her visits and see how things would turn out between us. Now I was becoming hopeful, but tried to keep calm.

Boss Lady said she would visit Little Lady's farm and check on me. She wanted to make sure this was the right place for me, especially after the last place turned out not to work out. I began to think maybe it had all worked out for the best in the long run as I liked Little Lady very much. Boss Lady explained she had already checked out Little Lady's farm and family. She felt everything was fine, but she stated adoption was a serious decision. She said she wanted me to become a member of a family, but wanted to make sure we were a good fit for each other.

She said she wanted us to be a happy family. Boss Lady explained that families can have difficulties and they have to work together to find solutions to problems. I thought if we loved and respected each other, and worked together, everything would be fine. Boss Lady also said since the adoption with Young Girl hasn't worked out, she didn't want me to be disappointed again. She wanted the best for me. I trusted Boss Lady and felt she would do whatever was right for me. I was getting very excited.

A few days passed. I tried to stay calm. I thought about Gus. I knew he would be happy for me. I still missed him a lot. Then Boss Lady told me that my adoption to Little Lady's family had been approved. I was happy, thrilled, excited, and nervous. I raced around telling everyone and saying my goodbyes. They were all happy for me.

Suddenly, a horse trailer with Cowboy Andy arrived and off I went to my new adoptive family.

PART #9

KAS GETS A NEW FAMILY

I was still nervous during the trip to my new home. I was eager to see Little Lady and the farm. Fortunately, the trip was short and we were soon there. The sign on the gate stated WELCOME TO TRANQUILITY RANCH. I thought that was a good name for my new home.

Little Lady was waiting for me in the yard when Cowboy Andy lead me out of the trailer. Little Lady walked me around the yard and into the barn. It was clean, neat, airy, and comfortable.

She told me I should relax, have a good night's sleep, and she'd show me around the farm in the morning. I thought this was a good idea because I was quite tired from all the excitement. I was already feeling content in my new home.

Out in the pasture, I noticed a black and white paint mare. She was beautiful. Was she my new sister? Would she be happy to have an older brother? She was running and romping all over the field. She would run at top speed, stop on a dime, whirl around, and run again. She seemed talented and energetic. I wondered if she could do "tricks" like me.

Then I heard funny noises from the other pasture. Suddenly, I saw two small donkeys running toward the fence. They were playing and tossing buckets around the field. They were gray and much smaller than the donkeys at my home farm. Seeing the donkeys made me feel even more that Tranquility Ranch was the place for me.

Later, I heard dogs barking and saw Little Lady taking two dogs for a walk. Two donkeys, two dogs, and now 2 horses. This seemed like a nice size family.

I had a good night's sleep at my new home and was feeling fine. Little Lady brought me my breakfast bright and early in the morning. After I finished my food, she took me into the pasture and we walked around Tranquility Ranch. I met a brown and white, paint, mare who looked quite energetic. Then I meet Stanley and Stella who were small donkeys.

After Little Lady went back in her house, we started to get to know each other. At first, we jumped around, then walked around, circled each other, and looked at each other. We were curious about each other. Shelley raced off to the other end of the pasture and went romping all over the place. I walked every inch of the pastures to get the lay out of the place. Stella and Stanley watched me for awhile. Soon they came over and starting walking with me. Then we romped and frolicked for awhile. Later, we settled down and relaxed. We walked around the pastures some more and soon we were grazing in the sunshine.

Shelley was the name of the mare. She bucked, romped, raced, and trotted all over the place. She seemed quite dynamic. The donkeys stayed with me for awhile and then wandered off by themselves. They appeared to keep their distance from Shelley and she ignored them.

The morning went by peacefully. Little Lady came out to the pasture several times and watched us. I guess she was checking to see how we were getting along together. I was relaxed and enjoying myself. Tranquility Ranch felt like the right place for me.

I was still wondering about Shelley. She stayed at the far end of the pasture and ignored us. Suddenly, she came roaring up to the front and quietly walked around by me. She followed me around, seemed relaxed, and content. Shelley began to get restless and started bucking. roaring around, and wanting to play. I didn't mind romping for awhile, but Shelley didn't want to stop. After she wore me out, she started chasing the donkeys. Finally, we settled into a calm and contented routine. I was feeling good about my adopted family.

A week later, we were all relaxing in the pastures. It was a sunny, comfortable day. Suddenly out of no where, Shelley began to tease me, nag me, and hassle me. She just wouldn't let up. I tried to be patient, but she was getting on my nerves. Stella and Stanley took off for the end of the pasture.

I did realize that it takes time to adjust to a new family member. Shelley had been the only horse at Tranquility Ranch and now she had to share the limelight with me. Apparently, the adjustment was not easy for her.

At first, I was confused and couldn't figure out what happened. Then I remembered that back at my family farm sisters and brothers would get cranky with each other. They would get on each other's nerves. I decided Shelley had turned into my "night-mare" sister. She constantly wanted to be the boss. I thought the nickname was true and funny, but Shelley did not agree.

Stella and Stanley thought all the commotion was funny. They were also glad she was hassling me and not them. They said Shelley was a "night-mare" to them before I arrived. She had tons of energy and never settled down. She wanted to treat me like I was a cow. She would try to chase, herd, and run me all over the fields. She'd say under her breath that I was the family adopted cow. Cows are fine, but I'm Kas, aka, Casanova. She could be fine and suddenly start calling me a cow again. She's say why did Little Lady adopt a cow to be with the family? Then she would laugh and laugh and laugh.

I couldn't figure her out. What was wrong? Then I found

the answer! I overheard Little Lady talking to Vet Lady when she came to the ranch to give us our regular checkups. They said Shelley had been a champion barrel racer. She had been a STAR. No wonder she was grumpy. She was bored, she missed being a star, and needed a job.

One lazy morning, I was relaxing in the pasture. Stella, Stanley, and Shelley were at the far end of the pasture. I was close to the barn. I noticed a car drive into the yard, a Cowgirl Lady got out, and she walked to the door of the house. The two of them talked in the yard for awhile and then came toward to the pasture. I was curious, so I sundered toward the gate and tried to be nonchalant. I slowly moved closer as I listened to what they were saying.

They were standing by the gate, and I heard the Cowgirl Lady say how pleased she was that Shelley was going to work at a summer horse camp for Teenagers. Shelley would be teaching them barrel racing. Also one of the camp trainers would be riding Shelley for barrel racing competitions. Shelley would go back to be a STAR. I knew she'd be happy. She was thrilled and excited.

Little Lady and Cowgirl Lady got Shelley. Then they saddled her for Cowgirl Lady to ride. Off they went all over the pasture. I could tell Shelley was having was having a wonderful time. Cowgirl Lady was a confident and experienced rider. It was fun watching them ride around the ranch. Shelley looked great. I realized she should be a STAR as she was extremely talented.

Shelley was a changed horse when she found out about her new job. We were surprised at her new self. She was excited, pleasant, cheerful, and and happy. She even said she would miss us. We reluctantly had to admit that we would miss her too. She always kept things on the ranch lively. I thought perhaps things would be dull without her.

The job was just what she needed as she had too much talent and energy just to hang around the ranch. Shelley said she would come back to visit us and tell us all about her adventures.

Soon Cowboy Andy arrived with his horse trailer. I knew he would take good care of Shelley. She hurried into the trailer and off she went to her new job. Shelley was finally happy. We were happy for her and for all of us too.

PART #10

NEW FAMILY MEMBERS

The ranch was quiet and peaceful, then I overheard Little Lady talking on her cell phone. She was walking around the pasture and I was following her. She said we were adopting two new members for our family. I wondered what they would be like?

However, I was puzzled. Little Lady's conversation raised questions in my mind. It sounded like our new family members were not horses or donkeys. Were they cows, or goats? I was stumped. Who was coming into our family?? Shelley had moved for a new job. Now what? Who was coming? What was in store for the Tranquility Ranch family?

A week passed and nothing happened, the ranch was quiet. Then the horse trailer and Cowboy Andy arrived early one morning. Two strange creatures came out of the trailer. I had never seen anything like them. There was a small one and a large one. Perhaps, they were mother and daughter? I had seen an ostrich a couple times. These looked a little like ostriches, but with hair.

I just stood there. I starred at them. What were these creatures? I kept watching and wondering. I could not figure them out. One thing I did know for sure, these creatures were NOT horses, donkeys. mules, goats, or cows.

I slowly moved closer to them. The large one stood in front of the little one and gave me an extremely hostile look. She was quite protective of the little one.

Stella and Stanley stood like statues. They were bewildered. The creatures looked odd, smelled odd, and sounded odd. The big one made funny noises. First the noise was a humming sound and then a weird yodeling noise. Later she made a sound that could have been for an alarm, because both of them ran to the far end of the pasture. I was intrigued.

Little Lady and Cowboy Andy were talking. After lots of practice, I had developed the nonchalant approach. This way I could get close and listen with no one paying attention to me. I picked up many interesting tidbits of information from this method. They said these creatures were Llamas. What? I had never heard of a Llama. Cowboy Andy was talking about them being pack animals in the Andes Mountains of Peru. He also said they were relatives of the Camel, but without a hump. He said further that that their hair is used to make clothes and blankets. They sounded to me more like a sheep than a camel.

After Cowboy Andy left and Little Lady went back into the house, we were still starring at each other. Slowly, we all began to walk in circles. Round and round we walked. It was like a weird dance routine. We walked in small circles and gradually the circles became bigger and bigger. We continued to look at each other as we circled each other. We never took our eyes off each other. Then slowly the circles began to get smaller and smaller. We got closer and closer to each other. After awhile, we all began to relax and were soon walking around together. Then we all went our separate ways and everything was calm on the ranch.

PART #11

LET'S HAVE SOME FUN!

After a short time, the ranch was calm and the days were uneventful. I thought we slowly decided that we could all get along together and be a family. The Tranquility Ranch was tranquil once again and we were all content together.

One day, I noticed that Home-Man's pick up truck was full of bales of hay. He had gone into the house and left the truck all alone. The ranch was quiet. I wandered over to the truck to check what else was in the truck. Sure enough, I could see the edge of my bag of food under the bales.

Well, I thought to myself, I could sure use a snack right about now. I quietly set to work moving the hay bales around the back of the truck. I was determined to get my snack. It wasn't easy. It took some time to move the bales, so I could get my snack.

I tried and tried, and finally, got my bag of food. Then I enjoyed my afternoon snack. Then I trotted to the far end of the pasture and put on my innocent look, but I was chuckling to myself.

When Home-Man and Little Lady came out of the house and discovered my accomplishment, they were not pleased and went grumbling around the yard. Home-Man yelled at me, but fortunately, I was far out in the pasture and couldn't hear a word of what he said. I did really enjoy my snack.

A week or two passed quietly, then one pleasant afternoon, I noticed the garage door was wide open. Both Home-Man's truck and Little Lady's car were parked in the yard. They both were in the house. I did my nonchalant approach and checked out the house to see what was happening. I think I think they must have been taking a nap. No one was in sight. The others were way out in the pastures. Everything were quiet. It seemed like a good time for me to visit the garage.

I quickly went into the garage. I looked around and spotted the refrigerator. I remembered Little Lady taking the carrots out of it a few days ago. I pulled the handle. Nothing happened. It was closed tight. I tried several more times and nothing happened. I pulled harder and the door popped open. I saw the carrots. There were lots of them! I wanted to cheer and tell the others, but I knew I'd better keep quiet. I started to laugh and had to control myself.

I got hold of a big bag and pulled it out to the fields. When everyone realized I had something, they all came running to see the stuff. I shared the carrots with everyone. They were excited. We had a fun party!

Suddenly, Home-Man came out of the house. He must have woke up from his nap. He was suspicious of us. He saw the bag and a couple carrots. At the moment, he really didn't know how we got the carrots, but he was upset anyway. We all chuckled. We thought the whole thing was funny. After all, things can happen when you doze off in the middle of the afternoon.

It did take him a while to figure out what happened with the carrots. Later in the day, he yelled at me to stay out of the garage. Then I realized I had forgotten to close the refrigerator door. I had gotten all excited over finding the carrots. I'm sure they'd have eventually figured it out anyway. However, whenever the group wanted a good laugh, someone mention the "carrot caper". Then we'd laugh and laugh.

We were getting along fine and things were calm. We were becoming a contented blended Family.

PART #12

WHAT NOW?

One day, a horse trailer drove into the yard. We were all surprised. I was nervous and concerned. I wondered what this would mean to our blended family? There was Cowboy Andy again. As usual, I was thinking, now what? What's happening? Oh no. here we go again!

Then I went into total shock and disbelief! I was speechless. The donkeys were braying at the top of their lungs. When they get going, they make a lot of noise. However, I couldn't blame them. Mama Llama started her danger alert sound. She and Spice took off quickly and went to the far end of the pastures.

Cowboy Andy opened the door of the trailer. I was in a complete state of shock. Why was this happening?? Why? Why? What is in store for us?

WHAT A SHOCK!!! There she was! SHE WAS BACK!!! The "night-mare" star, quarter horse. SHELLEY was back at Tranquility Ranch. Why? Now what?? She gave out a loud hello sound. We were all still too shocked to reply.

We then heard another loud hello from the trailer. We were shocked again. What is happening? A huge, high stepping, horse came out of the trailer. He looked confident and dignified horse.

My first thought was that these two would probably try

to take over the whole ranch and drive us crazy. I was getting exasperated. I was already uptight and anxious about their arrival.

We soon found out that Shelley and her friend were visiting only for a few weeks. Their home ranch family went to Hawaii for their vacation. This news was a relief to all of us!

Apparently, Little Lady and Shelley's home family thought it would be a good idea for her to visit us. They sent her friend along too. After I heard the details, I was able to relax.

Much to our surprise, Shelley seemed happy to be home again. She acted like a sister who came home for a visit. She introduced her friend, Reginald Sebastian Vance Quinn III. She said Reginald was from the Andalusian family of horses. She related these horses had originally lived on the Liberian Peninsula dating back 25,000 years. She said the horses were one of the rarest breeds in the United States. Of course, Shelley would have to have a rare friend.

At first, I wasn't sure what to think of Reginald, but he turned out to be quite pleasant. He told me to call him, Reggie. We had many good conversations and enjoyable times together. Shelley also turned out to be fun and more easy going than in the past.

The Llamas went their own way most of the time, but Stella and Stanley would always join in on the fun. We romped and frolicked in the pastures for hours. We did enjoy their visit after our initial shock and confusion wore off.

Shelley and I even had alone time together. She seemed enthused about her barrel racing job and had even won many prizes. She also confided to me that she now realized how nice it was to have a true friend. Someone who believes in you, cares about you, stands by you, and wants only the best for you. She said that Reggie and her are true friends forever. I was happy for her and realized how much I missed my friend, Gus.

PART #13

WHO's THIS?

We were sad to see Shelley and Reggie leave the ranch. We enjoyed their visit. It was nice to meet Reggie and to spend time with the new and improved Shelley. They had fun too, but were eager to get back to their jobs. Shelley had plans to win more prizes for barrel racing and Reggie for dressage.

The ranch seemed quiet and rather dull after Shelley and Reggie left. We slowly settled back into our usual routines. We were rested and relaxed, when out of nowhere, Cowboy Andy and his horse trailer arrived. Now What? I had no Idea what was happening now.

We all stood silently in the pasture and watched as Cowboy Andy opened the trailer door. Little Lady was in the yard watching too.

First, we heard a loud, deep, baritone sound. I mean very loud and very deep. Then he came out of the trailer. He brayed again. This time even louder. We all started to snicker. He brayed again, even louder. Bye now, we were all laughing uproariously. I was wondering what the neighbors were thinking. I was sure people could hear him in the next state. He was a big, sturdy, chocolate, donkey. I had never heard a donkey that loud.

Stella and Stanley were shocked. They were little donkeys. He was a giant compared to them. He was bigger and louder than both of them put together. The Llama were cautious as usual and kept their distance. We learned that he was a donkey rescued from Oklahoma. I thought the people in Oklahoma would still be able to hear him bray loudly.

Part # 14

HERE COMES MORE NEW FAMILY MEMBERS.

I laughed and laughed as I told everybody that maybe we should rename our ranch. I hadn't decided whether the name should be No Tranquility, Noisy Tranquility, or sometimes Tranquility Ranch. Little Lady called our new, loud, adopted, brother Double Dip after chocolate ice cream. I called him Double D, but I really wanted to call him Double L for double loud.

A few months passed and, suddenly, Cowboy Andy and his horse trailer came into the yard. This time he brought us two young rescue horses. They were handsome with the names of Cody and CD (cash on delivery), a Paso and a Quarter horse. They were frisky and devilish. They enjoyed romping around the pastures. They could be rebellious. I must admit that they often reminded me of myself in my younger days. I tried to teach them manners, but they didn't cooperate. Then Stella decided somebody had to teach them, so she took a firm hand with them and taught them proper pasture manners. We were all surprised, but they listened to her. It was a slow process, but she never gave up on them. They settled down and behaved much better. We were thankful for her efforts. I think Little Lady was glad too.

Suddenly, Cowboy Andy and his trailer arrived again. I loved Little Lady, but I thought she was going overboard with adoptions. Two more Llamas joined our family, Jerry and Koose. Jerry was white with brown patches and Koose was reddish brown. They played and romped together in the pastures, but were shy with us. It took time, but we settled into a contented routine.

Then one day a different horse trailer came into our yard. I looked for Cowboy Andy, but I didn't see him. This was strange. We couldn't imagine what was happening now. Cowboy Andy always came with the horse trailer.

Then a tall Cowgirl Lady got out of the trailer. Little Lady came out of the house to talk to the tall Cowgirl. Little Lady looked mighty short beside her. It made us chuckle at the tall and short persons standing together.

Cowboy Lady opened the trailer door and out came the littlest horse I had ever seen in my whole life. We all laughed when I said that Little Lady and the new little horse were the same height. He was black and white. We now had another new member of our blended family, making a total of 11, not counting the 3 dogs.

We could tell he wasn't a baby colt, but a tiny horse. I'd heard of miniature horses, but none of us had ever seen one. We were curious. Little Lady called him, Sammy. I used my nonchalant approach to listen to Cowgirl and Little Lady discussing him. Sammy was a rescue horse as his family couldn't take care of him anymore. He was young and needed a family. I thought we could be the right family for him. He was shy at first, but soon was one of the family. He seemed happy to be one of us.

Sammy enjoyed playing with all of us. He liked Cody and CD to chase him. He would run and run as he had lots of energy. He also enjoyed playing with Stella and Stanley. The Llamas kept a close eye on him and Double Dip would chase him from time to time.

Sammy was happy, energetic, fast, and easy going with everybody. Sammy followed each of us around the pastures from time to time. Stella and I taught him pasture manners and communication skills, plus danger and call for help signals. He learned fast, listened carefully, and made good progress.

Little Lady had a good time with the little one, especially since they were the same height. We laughed when little Stella, little Stanley, little Sammy and Little Lady worked in a line with the rest of us following them to go to the barn for our meals. We were quite an interesting blended family. We were getting along fine, had fun together, and Little Lady took good care of us.

As I roamed the pastures, I was pleased that Little Lady had found me at the Rescue Ranch. Now I had young family friends who kept the place lively. I never knew what they'd come up with next. Little Lady often had her hands full, but we all respected her and she was our leader. I often felt that it was my destiny to find Little Lady. I thought she had a special gift to work with animals.

If we'd ever move to a bigger ranch with more pastures, I knew she'd add even more of us to her family. Whoever she would decide to bring into our family, they'll be mighty lucky to be with us. I heard one visitor say that she wanted to "come back" as one of Little Lady's pets. I guess people realize what a good job Little lady does taking care of us. Are we really pampered and spoiled? All I know is that we are happy, content, and well nourished.

Part # 15

HAPPENINGS AT THE RANCH

There were now fourteen of us in our adoptive blended family: Stella, Stanley, Sammy, Mama Llama, Spice, Cody, CD, Double Dip, Jerry, Koose, and me, plus 3 dogs. We settled into a comfortable outline. Spice thought Coddy was wonderful and followed him everywhere. Generally, everyone got along fine.

I was grateful for my fanily, especially Little Lady. She took terrific care of us, and I felt that I had a special connection with her. She was a kind and caring person. I truly felt I would have been a dead horse, if it hadn't been for her. My senior citizen years had been comfortable and joyful because of her. I would never be able to adequately express my gratitude and love for her. I knew we would be in each other's hearts forever.

The Use-To-Be-Tranquil Ranch (my name for our home since the new arrivals) was located by a large, dry lake bed. The lake (Little Lady told visitors) had been dry for ten years . The lake had been swallowed up by a sink hole. Now that's weird. How could a sinking hole swallow a whole lake? It would have to be a mighty DEEP and DRY hole. As a result of the DEEP hole that sucked up all the water, we were lake front property with no lake. In fact. There were no signs of the lake ever coming back again. We had fenced pastures, plenty of areas to explore, and grass to eat. We were dry and content.

Then suddenly, the rains came to our ranch. It rained and rained and rained; day after day. Here came the hurricanes, one after another. There were five hurricanes with massive amounts of rain. Water was everywhere and the LAKE WAS BACK. Now we were the Underwater-Waterlogged Ranch. We all had to move closer to the house where the land was mostly dry. The lake had over flowed onto our pastures and we became part of the lake. Now we needed that sink hole to suck some of the water off our pastures. I did not want to swim around the ranch. However, the sink hole was no help. We were cozy and dry near the house and barn, but the rest of the land was LAKE.

One afternoon, I was leisurely walking around the yard when I saw something strange in our part of the lake. It looked like a small headed lake creature moving in the water. Everyone yelled when they spotted the creature. We were all puzzled. Where had the creature come from and what was out there in the water?

We watched and watched. Maybe the creature came from the lost sink hole. The head was moving around the lake. The creature was looking calmly here and there. Then we saw the head and a long neck coming out of the lake. We all started to yell. Then we started to laugh. We laughed and laughed hysterically. We couldn't stop laughing. IT WAS SPICE!! What a devilish young Llama! Spice was laughing as she came running full speed out of the lake. She had enjoyed her swim in the lake and the uproar she caused with us all.

Finally, the excitement settled down and we were relaxing, but still chuckling over the episode. Later, I noticed Spice lying flat out on the ground sound asleep. I figured she was tired after her swim. Cody came over and stated nudging her, but she was still sleeping.

Suddenly, Little Lady came running out of the house yelling loudly. She was running so fast she was almost flying. Everyone started to make loud noises too. We didn't know what was happening. Spice woke up and looked around bewildered. All the noise and uproar had startled her. She had been sound asleep. Then I realized Little Lady had thought something was wrong with Spice since she flat on the ground zonked out from her swim.

We knew Little Lady was a caring person and we all loved her dearly, but we all had to laugh at this situation. Little Lady was greatly relieved that Spice was fine.

Of course, the next day Cody had to go into the water and try swimming too. Fortunately, he took his nap standing under a tree and didn't cause Little Lady any anxious moments.

One day, I decided to check out what was happening on the house porch. I thought the porch stoop would be the prefect place for me to stand, observe, and listen. I used my nonchalant approach as I slowly went up the steps to the porch. If some one would open the door I could walk right onto the porch, then into the living room. I was doing fine.

However, Home-Man saw me and flipped out. He yelled for Little Lady who came running to the screen door. She made me get off the stoop and brawled me out. She said I could hurt myself. I realize she looks out for my welfare, but I liked being on the stoop. However, now it is off limits for me. She put a barrier across the steps to make sure I don't try again.

I have my various tricks of opening doors, opening gates, opening refrigerators, opening bags of food, and my nonchalant approach to finding information of interest to me.

Of course, I liked the porch stoop and the garage, both are not allowed now. I also liked to kick the gates, especially when I got hungry. Home-Man always yelled at me when I kicked the gate, but I decided to ignore him as I was just expressing myself, asking for food, wanting attention, or upset about something. Also I must admit that at times I just kicked the gates because it was fun. I even taught Cody how to kick the gate. Cody was a fast learner and does a good job. I was

happy and having fun, but I did realize I was living with a
bunch of kids.

PART #16

SURPRISE!!

Youngsters can be entertaining, but they can wear you to a frazzle and complete exhaustion. I was deeply thankful for all my blessings, but I still had a longing for a friend of my own age. I was at a different stage of my life now. I wanted some adult conversation and relaxation time with a friend. I was even beginning to miss Shelley and Reggie.

It was one of those days when the youngsters were especially rambunctious. They were frolicking all over the pastures and having a grand time. I was dozing under a tree. Suddenly, I heard a noise. I looked around and I saw a horse trailer coming into the yard. We were all shocked! I could tell it wasn't Cowboy Andy's trailer and we were even more surprised.

Little Lady came out of the house. I wanted to tell her that we did not need any more kids on our ranch.

Then a Cowgirl came out of the trailer cab. She and Little Lady talked for awhile. I walked to the far end of the pasture and turned my back to the trailer. I did not want to see the new youngster. I was already out numbered nine to one. I watched the sunset and tried to take my mind of the horse trailer.

I heard the trailer's door open. I heard some other noises and then a horse whinny. The sound was vaguely familiar. I was caught off guard. I wondered what was going now?

As I slowly turned around, the new horse whinnied again, but this time much louder. I knew I had heard that sound before somewhere.

Then I saw the horse.

I was in a complete state of shock.

I was speechless. I was frozen in place.

I could not move. I could not believe my eyes. Was I imagining this? Was I dreaming? Was this true? I was still completely in shock.

There standing in middle of our yard was a handsome, gray, senior citizen horse.

IT WAS GUS!!!! My best ever friend was right here in our yard.

He started to gallop towards me. I still could not believe he was really here. I was excited and and thrilled. Gus was right here in person standing in front of me. Face to face. Nose to nose. We were filled with jubilation and excitement. I could tell he was just as thrilled to see me as I was to see him. I suddenly realized how much I had missed him.

IT WAS A MIRACLE TO ME!!!

We could hardy talk with were so excited.

Gus explained that Tall Lady had started her own business and would be traveling all over the place. She didn't want Gus to be home all alone. She knew he would be lonely, so she talked to Little Lady. They made arrangements for Gus to live with us. This way she could come to visit Gus and me too.

It was exciting to see Gus, but even more exciting to learn he was going to live with us. This was wonderful! Now we had eleven in our ranch family and I had my buddy with me. We can watch the youngsters together as we relax and enjoy ourselves.

I remembered what Shelley had told me. Now I knew exactly what she meant about having a friend. It is truly wonderful to have a true friend. I'm a happy, happy horse! I have Little Lady, my blended family, and my friend, Gus.

KAS PROVERBS FOR FRIENDS AND FAMILY
PART #1

1. Never give up.

2. Your Friends will respect you for who you are, bring out the best in you, and encourage your positive attributes.

3. You can handle your challenges. Keep trying and believe in yourself.

4. Friendship is a two-way street.

5. Appreciate yourself and your friends.

6. There'll be a caring soul ready to help you, when you really need help.

7. Giving up is not an option.

8. Walk on the bright side of life.

9. Forgive and move on with your life.

10. Dwell on the positives.

11. Concentrate on your own life and let others be free to live their own.

12. Appreciate your blessings.

KAS PROVERBS -
PART # 2

1. Laugh. Laugh. Laugh. Be happy. have fun, enjoy life.

2. Laugh till tears roll down your cheeks.

3. Smlle at others. Put some cheer into their lives.

4. If you grin at others - do they then look at you suspiciously? Are they thinking - why Is that person grinning? (Good!)

5. Laughter Is contagious!

6. The family that laughs together, stays a family.

7. Marriage without laughter is like ham without eggs.

8. Friends laugh together.

9. Dating without laughter is dull.

10. A hearty laugh a day, keeps the doctor away.

11. Laughter at work Is good for morale.

12. Laugh at the absurdities of life.

13. Laughter before bedtime, helps for a peaceful sleep.

14. Life can be humorous.

15. See the humor all around you.

16. Familles, couples, friends who laugh together, want to be together.

INFO

Send your email for Kas to: blazlyahoo.com

If you want to write to Kas. send your mail to:

P.O. Box 770864, Ocala, FL 34477-0864

****

Want to help rescued horses?

CONTACT:
Horse Protection Association
20690 N W 130th Avenue
Micanopy, Florida 32667

Website: www.hpaf.org

****

Learn how to train your horse: check out the book "NATURAL
HORSE*MAN*SHIP" by Pat Parelli and visit his website
at: www.parelli.com